How to Draw
DINOSAURS

Learn to draw 20 prehistoric creatures, step by easy step, shape by simple shape!

Illustrated by Jeff Shelly

GETTING STARTED

When you look closely at the drawings in this book, you'll notice that they're made up of basic shapes, such as circles, triangles, and rectangles. To draw any dinosaurs, just start with simple shapes, as you see here. It's easy and fun!

CIRCLES are used to draw this dino's chest, hips, and "sail."

 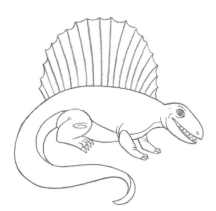

RECTANGLES are good for drawing blocky or boxy heads on dinosaurs.

TRIANGLES are best for drawing dinos with pointed heads.

TIPS

When you're ready to bring your prehistoric creatures to life on paper, use crayons, markers, or pencils. Because no one really knows what dinosaurs looked like, get creative with greens, oranges, purples, or blues!

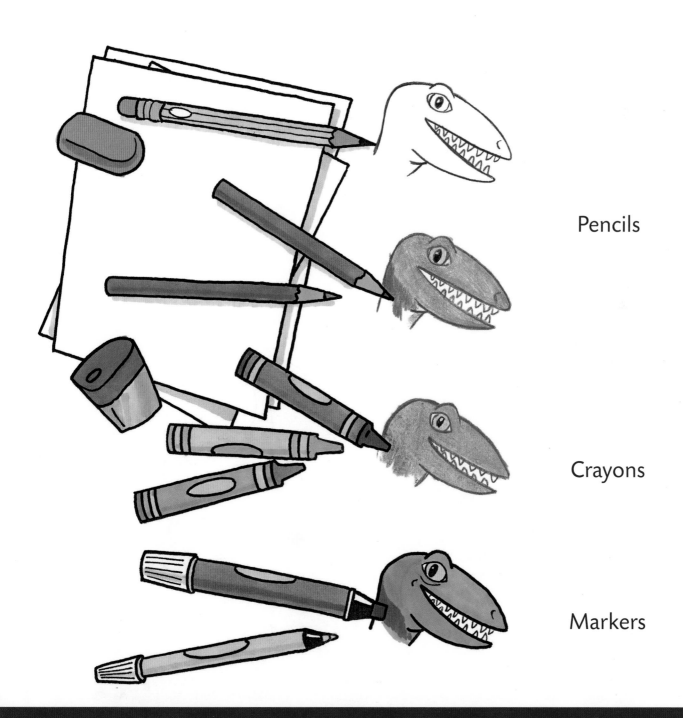

Pencils

Crayons

Markers

ORNITHOMIMUS

ornithomimus means "bird mimic," so it should come as no surprise that this dinosaur's neck and legs were shaped like those of an ostrich!

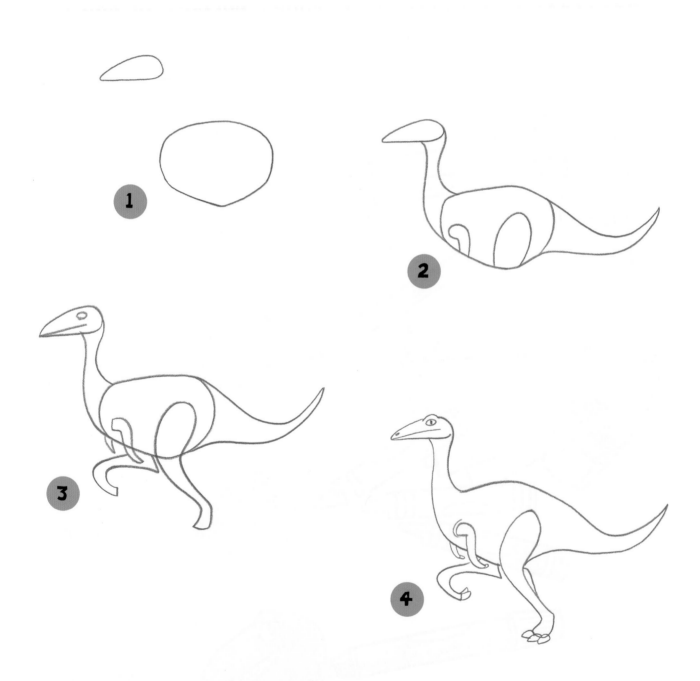

5

6

MYTH

All dinosaurs lived at the same time.
Fact: In the 165 million years from the dinosaurs' first appearance 230 million years ago to their "disappearance" 65 million years ago, many different species coexisted—but not every species existed during the same time period.

PROTOCERATOPS

The slow-moving Protoceratops was heavy and round. It relied on a thick helmet and pointed beak to fight off predators.

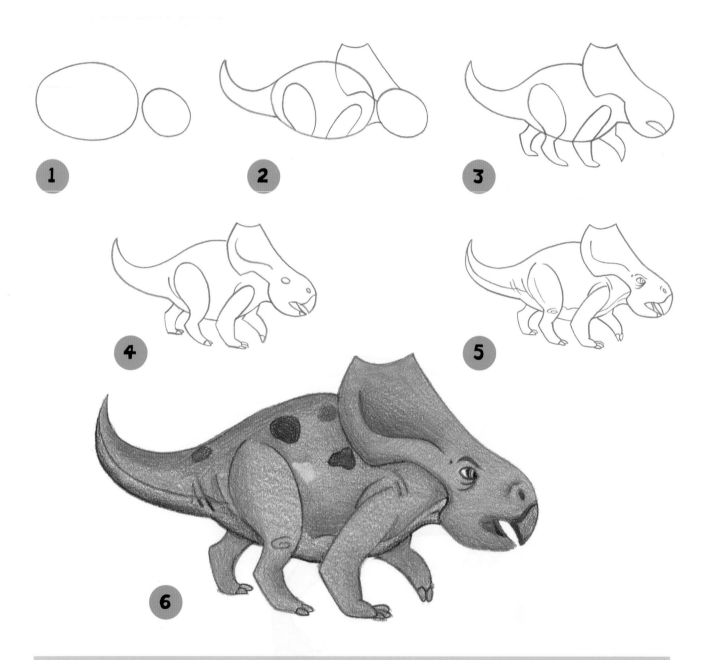

1

2

3

4

5

6

IGUANODON

The Iguanodon walked on all fours, but it could stand briefly on its strong back legs and use its "hands" to gather food.

BRACHIOSAURUS

With tall legs, a long neck, and large nostrils
on its head, this plant eater was able to find leaves
and fruit that other dinos couldn't reach.

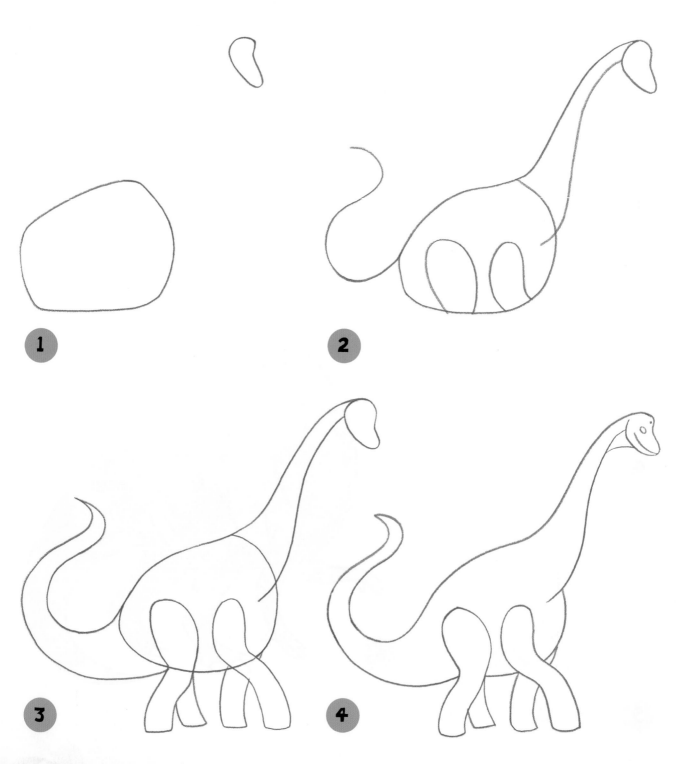

FUN FACT

The Brachiosaurus is a sauropod, one of a group of large plant-eating dinosaurs with long necks and tails and small heads. Most sauropods have front legs that are much shorter than their hind legs. But the Brachiosaurus has longer front legs, which is why the scientists gave it a name that means "arm lizard"!

5

6

QUETZALCOATLUS

There was more to this flying lizard than wingspan!
The Quetzalcoatlus had a compact,
bean-shaped body, a long neck, and a beak.

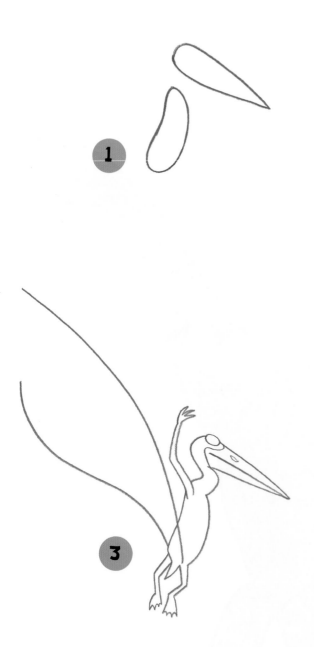

MYTH

There were 700 types of dinosaurs.
Fact: Experts have identified about 700 different dinosaurs, but there may have been many more. After all, in 1842, we knew of only 3 dinosaurs: Megalosaurus, Iguanodon, and Hylaeosaurus!

5

6

FUN FACT

Scientists know the Quetzalcoatlus was a carnivore, but they still can't agree on exactly what it ate. Some say it swept down on dead dinos like a vulture. Others claim it fed like a pelican, plucking fish from shallow seas.

STYRACOSAURUS

To draw the heavy Styracosaurus, begin with a heart-shaped head and a round body. Later be sure to add its horn and six-spike frill.

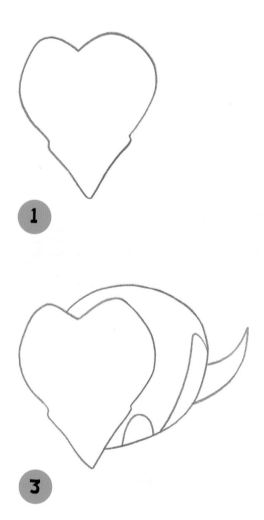

1

2

3

4

FUN FACT

The Styracosaurus resembled the Protoceratops and the Triceratops because they were all members of the same family: ceratopians. One of the last dino groups to evolve, ceratopians were large, horned plant eaters that moved together in herds.

5

6

7

8

TROÖDON

Lightweight and quick, the Troödon was a master carnivore. It was named "wounding tooth" for its mouth full of sharp, jagged teeth!

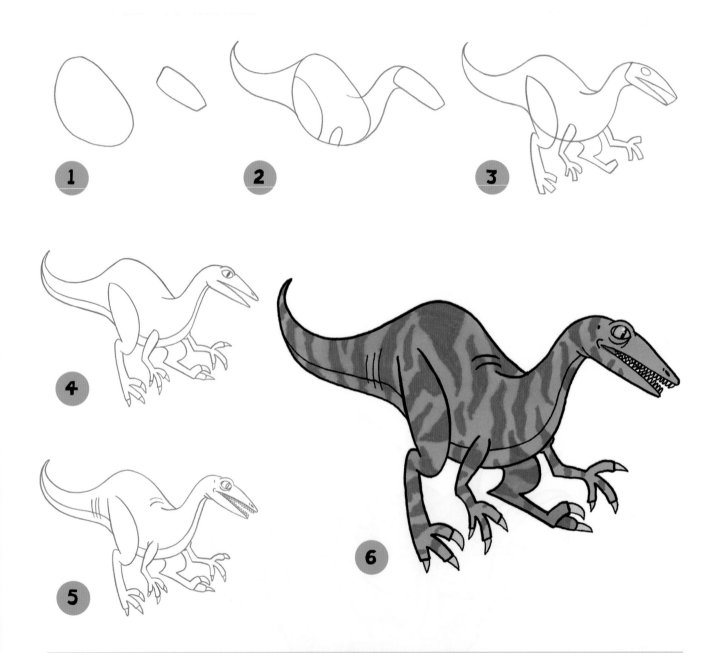

1

2

3

4

5

6

FUN FACT

The Troödon was a biped, meaning that it walked on two feet. Standing tall, this dinosaur's height ranged from 6.5 to 11 feet (2 to 3.35 m). But because of its hollow bones, the Troödon probably weighed only about 110 pounds (50 kg).

ALLOSAURUS

Draw this sauropod-eating carnivore with a strong neck, sturdy legs, and a powerful tail. Don't forget the sharp teeth and claws!

MYTH

The first humans lived at the same time as the dinosaurs.
Fact: The first human didn't appear on earth until about 62 million years after the last of the non-avian dinosaurs disappeared.

PTERANODON

The Pteranodon was a flying lizard with a tiny sausage-shaped body; a thin, long head with a birdlike beak; and large, batlike wings.

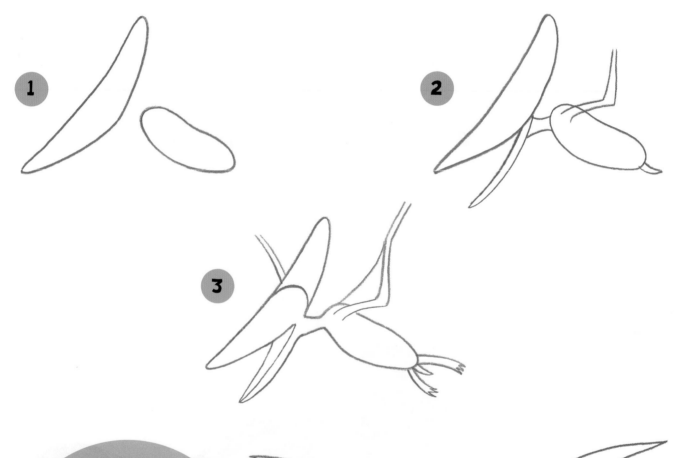

MYTH

An asteroid killed the dinosaurs.
Fact: The latest evidence shows that a large asteroid hit the earth right around the time of the dinosaurs' extinction. But most dinosaur experts believe this is just one of many reasons the dinosaurs died out.

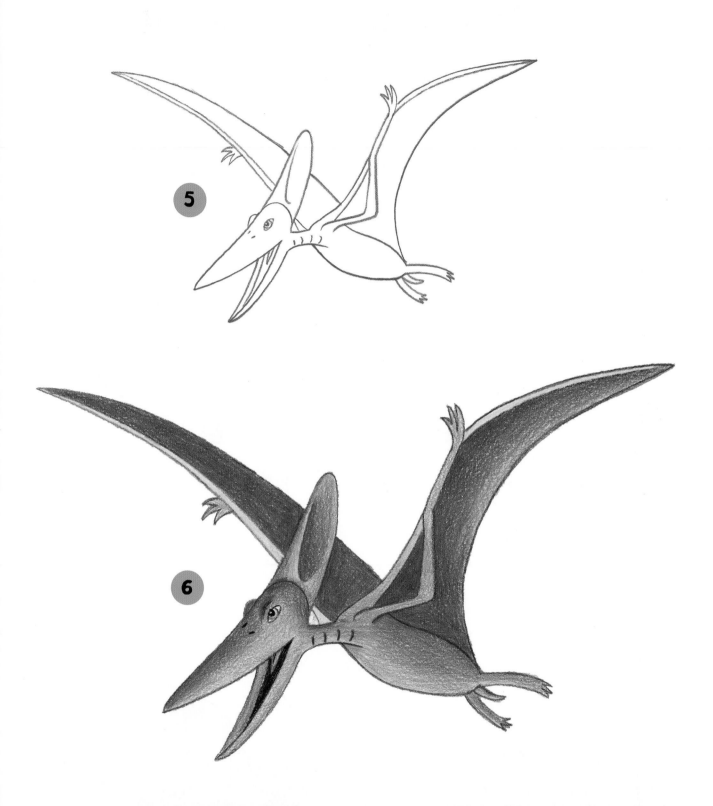

5

6

FUN FACT The Pteranodon belonged to the pterosaurs, a family of flying lizards that lived at the same time as the dinosaurs. Even though it had lightweight bones, the Pteranodon still weighed 37 pounds (17 kg). This non-dino needed wings that were 23 feet (7 m) wide to keep it airborne!

PARASAUROLOPHUS

Many dinos had heavy, thick bodies like the Parasaurolophus. But this biped's curved head crest and duck-billed beak made it unique!

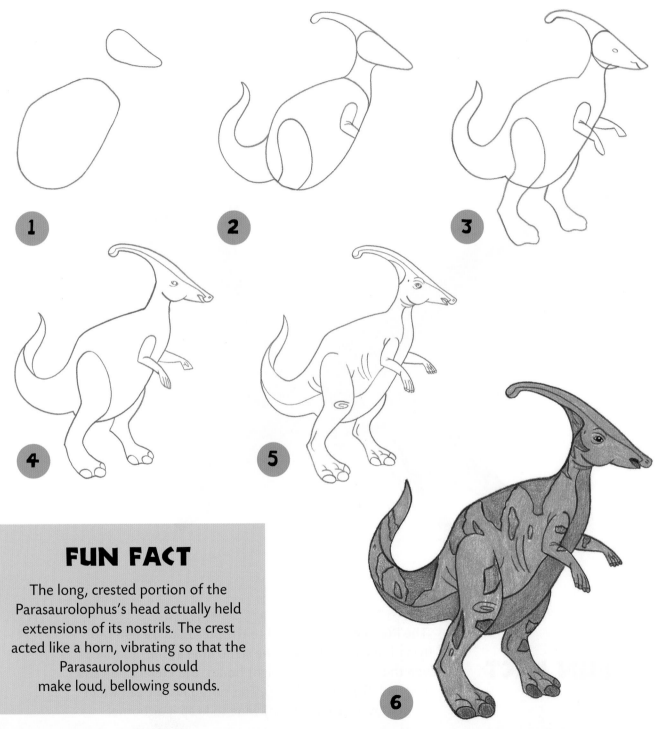

FUN FACT

The long, crested portion of the Parasaurolophus's head actually held extensions of its nostrils. The crest acted like a horn, vibrating so that the Parasaurolophus could make loud, bellowing sounds.

DIPLODOCUS

Draw this enormous sauropod with a large, oval body and a whiplike tail, but make its head small—it had a brain the size of a human fist!

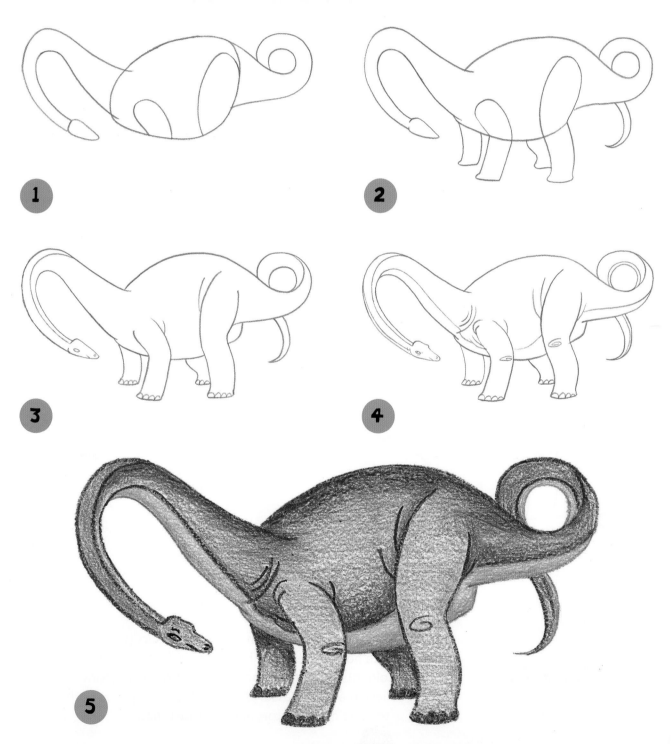

STEGOSAURUS

If you can draw your attention away from the row of plates on this stegosaur's back, you might notice its other features—including long, straight hind legs and a powerful, spiked tail.

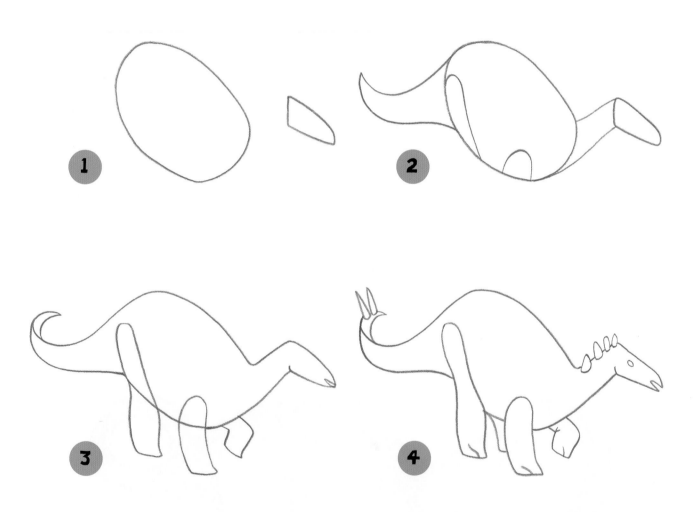

FUN FACT

The Stegosaurus is the largest of the stegosaurs (that is, dinos with bony plates, long hind legs, and small heads). Paleontologists—scientists who study life from prehistoric times—believe that a Stegosaurus would display its plates both to scare off predators and to attract mates.

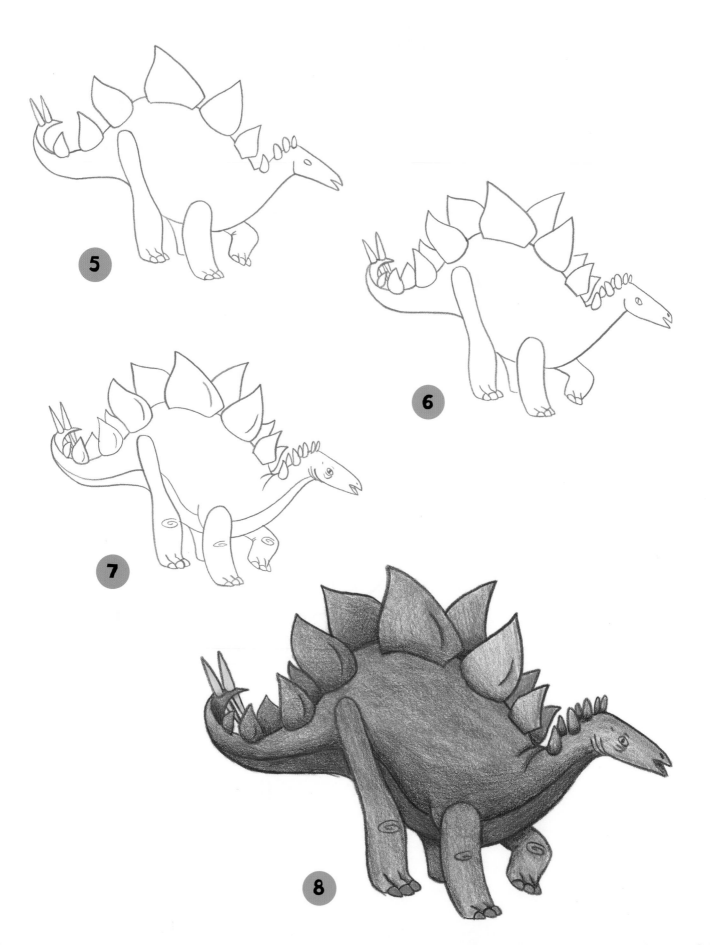

MAMENCHISAURUS

The Mamenchisaurus had the longest neck
of all the dinos! Its tail and body were also long,
but its legs were relatively short.

FUN FACT

Unlike most plant eaters today, the teeth of the Mamenchisaurus were not used to grind plant matter. Instead, they were used to strip off leaves, which the dinosaur then swallowed whole.

VELOCIRAPTOR

Velociraptor means "speedy predator," so it makes sense that this dino had a slim body, sharp claws, and a powerful jaw.

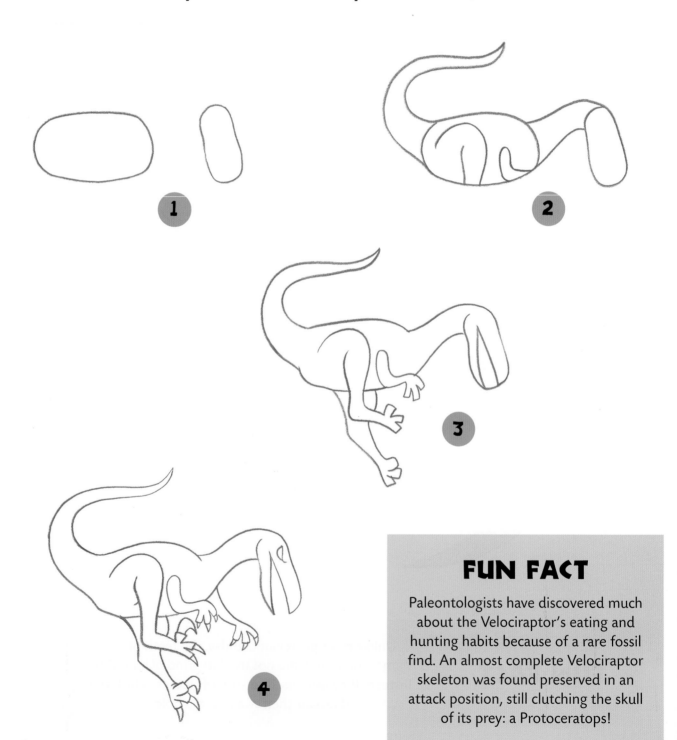

FUN FACT

Paleontologists have discovered much about the Velociraptor's eating and hunting habits because of a rare fossil find. An almost complete Velociraptor skeleton was found preserved in an attack position, still clutching the skull of its prey: a Protoceratops!

5

6

DIMETRODON

This spiny, sail-backed carnivore was
a pelycosaur, a prehistoric animal that roamed
the earth long before the dinosaurs.

1

2

3

4

5

6

UTAHRAPTOR

When referring to dinosaurs, raptor means "robber." This thief was a predator with powerful, clawed feet and long, grasping hands.

FUN FACT

In 1991, paleontologists in Utah uncovered the ultra-large Utahraptor. This striking dinosaur was 16 to 23 feet (4.8 to 7 m) long and weighed up to 1 ton!

TRICERATOPS

The bulky Triceratops is best known for its three horns. Draw one long horn above each eye and a third, shorter horn above the snout.

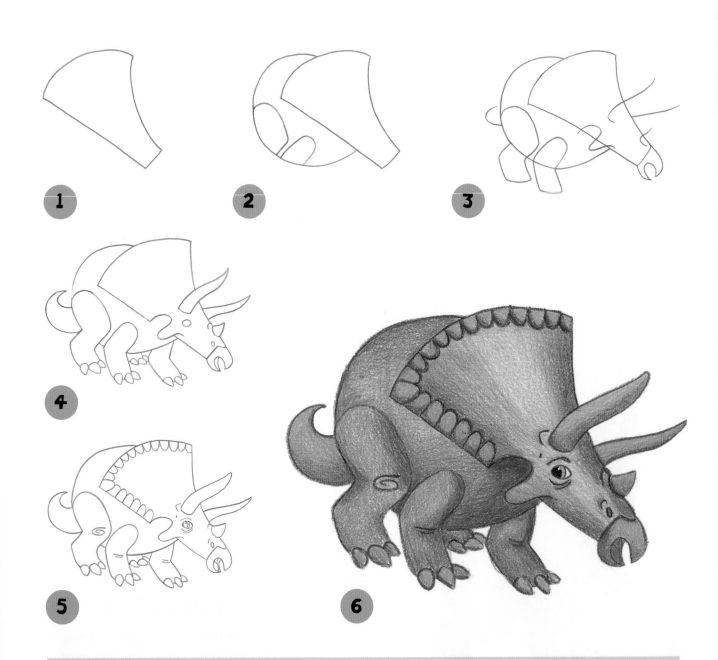

1

2

3

4

5

6

FUN FACT

Its three large horns gave the Triceratops a frightening appearance. But this herbivore probably would have used its horns only to defend itself—or to push over tall trees so it could reach taller branches with tender, delicate leaves.

PACHYCEPHALOSAURUS

The defining feature of this herbivore was its unusual head. Nine inches of bone protected the Pachycephalosaurus's brain. And the special bumps and nodes on its snout helped it root up food.

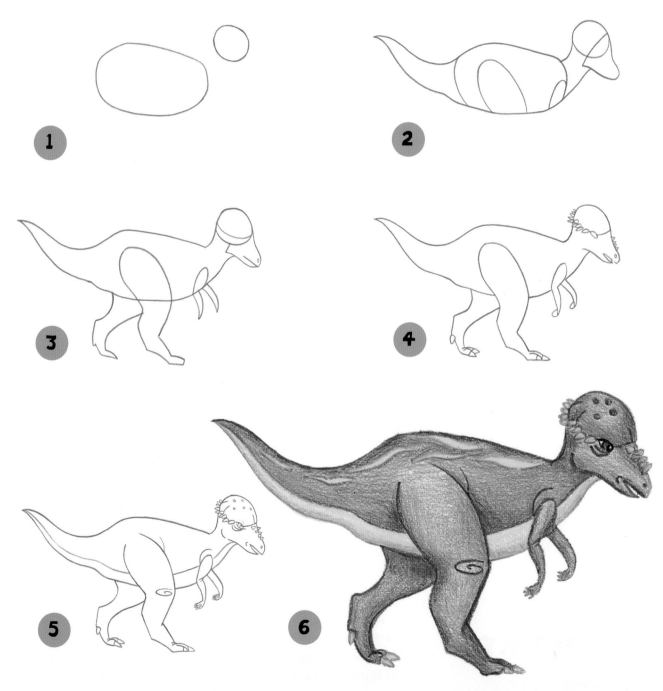

TYRANNOSAURUS

The largest in the family of bipedal carnivores known as theropods, the T-Rex had a big head, powerful legs, and a thick tail.

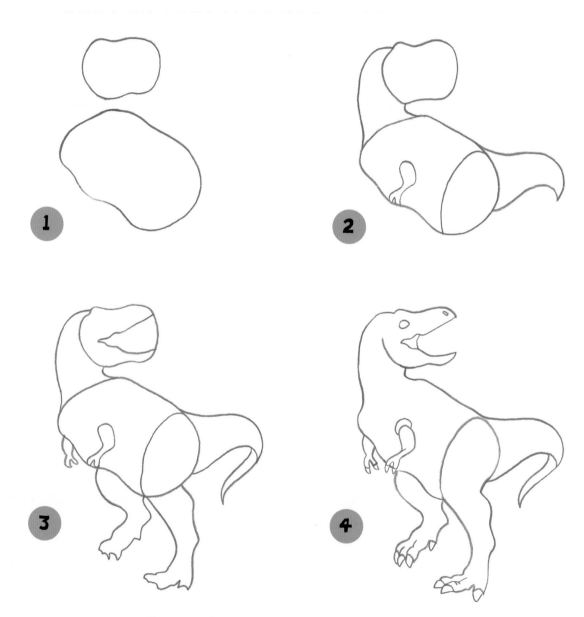

FUN FACT

The arms of the Tyrannosaurus were no laughing matter. Although they seem tiny compared to the rest of the "tyrant lizard," its two-fingered arms were at least three times as strong as human arms. And they were used as meat hooks!

5

MYTH

The first dinosaurs
were found in
the United States.
Fact: The first dinosaur
fossils to be scientifically
recorded were found in
Great Britain in the
early 1800s.

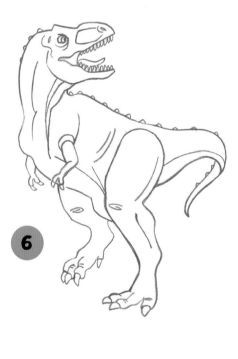

6

7

POLACANTHUS

Polacanthus means "many-spined", and there's no better way to describe this four-legged, tough-exterior dinosaur!